WET
PAINT
AND
OTHER
SIGNS OF
LOVE

—

LOIS
WYSE

Thomas Y. Crowell Company
Established 1834
New York

Designed and illustrated by Richard A. Voehl.

Manufactured in the United States of America.

Library of Congress Cataloging in Publication Data

Wyse, Lois.
Wet paint and other signs of love.
I. Title.
PS3573.Y74W44   811'.5'4   75-25500
ISBN O-690-01030-3

Here it is, my dear,
Another layer peeled —
And so we go
One step closer to the truth.

CONTENTS

WET PAINT

In the park
I like so much
There is a bench
And over it there is a sign:
Wet Paint.

       Do not sit.
       Do not touch.
       Do not disturb.

I was born under that sign.

       For there are days I cannot function in your life.
       There are times I am Wet Paint.

But do remember this, my love,
When I seem freshly striped:
Wet paint dries faster in the sun,
And you must learn to un-
derstand that even in the warmth of all your love
There still are times my paint is slow to dry.
So give me time, and meanwhile

       Do not sit.
       Do not touch.
       Do not disturb.

I need new paint.
I also need the sun.

PRIORITIES

Oh ye who drink of instant coffee,
Oh ye who take too many trips,
Oh ye who brush your teeth with commuter timetables,
Hurry to another un-meeting in a non-day
And hum numbers in a telephone
One two three six times to go.
How can you nourish all your day
With sweet and tender actions
If you never take the time
To do unimportant things?
Oh, my love, when did you last
See the dawn
And eat, one by one,
Red raspberries for breakfast?

WHAT'S THE MATTER?

What bothers you, my love?
What worries scorch the cool facade of you?
Tell me. Tell me.
I am not here
To darn your sox and ride the coattails of your life.

Talk a little, love,
And we will find a little love.

ANNE SEXTON

They played an Anne Sexton interview
On public TV tonight
And there she was
Dead dead Anne Sexton
Big as life talking larger than life
Out of death.

"Do you know yourself better when you write?"
 Asked the interviewer.
"No," she said, "my poetry knows more
 Than I do."

Dead dead Anne Sexton
With the hot living poetry
That burns my throat to read.
Dead dead Anne Sexton
With the living words scrawled on screaming orange paper.
I know me better reading you, Anne Sexton.
Why couldn't you hear your voice?
Were you kept alive by your shouting
And killed by your deafness?

OFF DAY

You had a sound
I recognized
On the telephone today.

It was that
"Even though you won't do what I want I'll survive thank you anyway"
Voice.

I know that voice very well, my love.
Wasn't it just yesterday
That I used it with you?

SHORT MEMORY

I cannot make my bed with memories,
So do not lend me yours.
I cannot live on past encounters.
Please do not tell me yours.
I am here and now and present,
Fresh and scrubbed and new.
But if that is so,
Why do I still cry at sunsets?

THE FIDELITY GAP

Fidelity went out of fashion
With virginity.
Or maybe it was the other way around.
No matter.
Most people really do not care
If you're in the sack with somebody else's someone
So long as you have the required number of orgasms
And perform the ritual foreplay.

Sex by the book has replaced
Love by the individual.

But oh, my dear, let me tell you something,
If you touch another woman,
Don't tell me.

If you take up with a lady steeplejack
Or leave your heart in San Francisco
I don't want to know.

It's not that I expect you to be faithful.
It's just that I couldn't love you if you weren't.

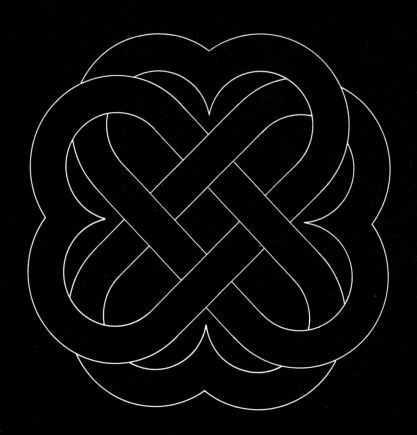

POWER

In the room I call my mind
You sit at one end
And sing madrigals
While I
Sob and sigh.

For you, sweet one, are part of that long line
Of men
Who own the world. You have
All the money and the guns and the power.
And I have a dust mop
And a two-piece bathing suit.

So you jingle the cash and load the guns and pound your fist
And think that makes me love you
When all the time the only thing that makes me love you
Is the madrigal
In my head
Just like the one I hear you sing.
Nice man, nice man,
Don't you know where your power really is?

ALL THE BEST MEN ARE MARRIED

He le
Down went the elevat
And back to the sure wor
Of, "What do you want to eat
And, "The electrician came today
No doubt
No uncertaint
Unless, of cours
He sometimes wonde
What she does aft
He leave

TO SOMEBODY ELSE

And she is left,
Down goes her heart.
Should she put on her clothes
And get something to eat?
Or wait. And maybe
Someone will call.
But it will not be his call.
For she is the daytime number.
The pit stop.
The place for quick drinking and love-by-the-clock until
She is left.

THE CELEBRATED BEAUTY

I lunched today with a celebrated beauty.
>She ate cold sea bass and asparagus, sipped white wine
>And said she never dieted.
We talked about the things
All women talk about today:
>The headlines in the morning paper,
>Tennis and other outdoor games,
>And in between she said how good her husband made her feel.
Eventually the talk turned to women
And the things that give a woman confidence.
>Money?
>Looks?
>Brains?
>I asked what she believed.
She smiled her famous red-lip smile and said:
>There is an actress, very famous,
>Who is probably the most beautiful woman in the world.
>She is in Europe now to divorce her husband.
>Why?
>Because, my dear, he cannot keep his eyes and hands off
>Every 20-year-old woman that he sees.
>So she is shaken, frightened,
>Because even the most beautiful woman in the world
>Needs the only thing that gives a woman confidence:
>The uninterrupted interest of just one man.
She smiled her famous red-lip smile and said:
>And that is what I finally have.

Ah, my celebrated beauty,
No wonder you never need to diet.

SERMON IN SAND

I ran across
The sand
And
Could not find
A single shell.

Then
I stood
In one place
And found seven.

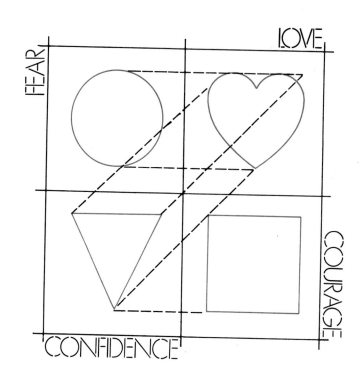

NO BRAVE LOVERS

Out of fear
Comes love.
Out of love
Comes confidence.
Out of confidence
Comes courage.

Courage is
Two steps
Removed from love.
Which is why
There are no brave lovers
Only scared ones.

LATER, LATER, ASK ME LATER

Sometimes we feel very close
To one another
At the very same moment.
For instance,
We're both reading,
And all of a sudden we look up,
And we find each other,
And at times like that
I might even lose my place in the book.

But sometimes I look up
And you don't.
I mean you go on reading
Or watching television
Or thinking 2,000-mile-away thoughts,
And I can't get through.

You look at me
Through plate glass eyes.

Hello hello it's me it's me.

No answer.

At times like that
Love is not so terrific
And I could get very disgusted
If I didn't remember one little phrase
You taught me long ago,
"Mutual does not mean simultaneous."

THE PRIVATE PERSON

Baked in an enameled shell of privacy,   I weep, I rage, I care.   Yet outside I am smooth, controlled.

Please do not come too close. Enamel chips so easily.

HOW DO YOU FEEL ABOUT ME?

"How do you feel about me?"

"Uneasy."

Wait a minute—just a minute—stop.
Whoever said it would be easy?
Where did you get the idea
That turning your life inside out would be a snap?
Who promised you it would be simple
To fall in love with a complicated person?
What wide-eyed ingenue promised you
Kisses and hugs and no minor arthritic pains?
Me?
What do you mean me?
How could it have been me?

I'm so uneasy
I have to ask how you feel about me.

NANTUCKET FOG

I remember morning
On Nantucket
When I saw the fog
Deny the day
Its right to brightness.

I thought about the fog on Nantucket
With us.
We are so careful to be cautious
That we try to let no fog obscure us from each other.
Yet it is only natural
For day…and me…and you…to have some secrets.

So let the fog roll in.
Although I cannot see you always,
I can feel that you are there
And behind the full grey skirts,
We, like the sun,
Can gather strength
And burn the fog between us.

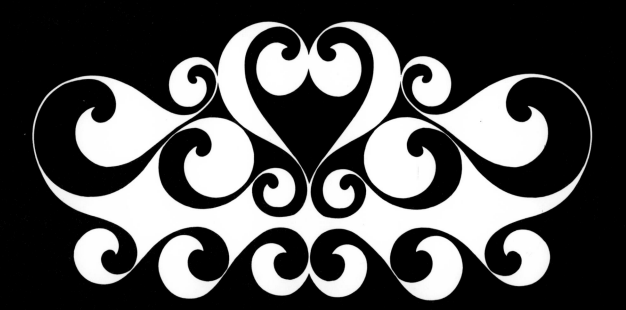

DEEP WATER

One step I took
Along a path
I never meant to walk.
One step was all I took.
One step and then another,
And now I find
The water's fine
Although I cannot see the shore.

But who needs to see the shore?
In deep water I am home.

NOTHING HAPPENS IN A MARRIAGE

You could not say it was a lover's quarrel.
We did not throw pots or words or knives.
All that came between us was
A silent time.

Even loves as old as ours.
Cannot live in silent times.
We need the sound of
Things we do not want to hear.

For we who thrive on talk, sweet talk,
Grow stronger still when we survive
The explosion of
A different kind of love.

In the mirror of my mind
I reflect on
Long, thin images
Of us.

I see you now.
Pensive and worried maybe,
Unsure of where we're going,
And I long to say to you,

"It does not matter where we're going.
I know where we have been.
I trust you.
I am the mirror image
Of your dreams."

THE MIRROR

In the mirror of my mind
I reflect on
Long, thin images
Of us.

I see you now.
Pensive and worried maybe,
Unsure of where we're going,
And I long to say to you,

"It does not matter where we're going.
I know where we have been.
I trust you.
I am the mirror image
of your dreams."

A PRIVATE WORLD

There are those
Who cannot bear to be
Alone.
But I can understand
The separations,
The long apartness
The "where are you's"
Of this, my unfilled life
Because
I have created
A private world
Where we never are apart.
Beating always in my head
Is your heart.

HOLDING PATTERN

This is the moment I would like to hold
Long after other times are
Forgotten,
Pushed aside and
Filed in some wistful webbing
We call memory.

This is the moment I would like to hold,
My love,
Not by remembering it,
But by reliving it.

OCIAL SUCCESS

ing
ing
onversa-
on
op
ril-
ant
eople.

h, what a smashing group we cast
or this small dinner party.
ow it is late.
nd the
ing
ing
op

       Did you bolt the door?
       Are the glasses in the sink?

rilliant
eople
Iave gone home,
nd we are left
o tidy up their thoughts.

       Let the ice melt down the side
       Of the alumidumdum bucket.

think that someone lost
wo buttons and a thread of conversation,
But I am too tired to match buttons,
And I like our threads better.

       Come closer, won't you, love?
       The dishes will wait,
       But why should we?

HEARTFELT

We have made giant strides in loving,
You who never knew of love,
And I who knew it all.

So now you know that love does not have birthdays,
And I know that what has been can be again
If we both will wish it so,

And oh, my love, I wish it so.
I am back to knit one purl one
In the pattern of life

And somewhere in this confusing crazy quilt
I clearly see
The heartprints of our love.

CITY LOVES

Some people think that love is quite idyllic.
They set love in a pastoral place
Just a little east of imagination and west of reality
And there in a never-never land of clear blue skies
Expect the love to grow.

But I have learned
There is no proper setting for a love that works,
For taxi horns
Can sound the call to love
And city streets can heat
Because of us.

HOT AND COLD RUNNING CONVERSATION

When the telephone rang,
I knew it would be the plumber
So I gathered my stopped sink voice and said,
"Hello."

"Hello," you said,
"Does my voice sound familiar?"

Familiar? (Small laugh. Me.)
Familiar. (Bigger laugh. You.)

A few words
And then
Quick clicks.

Now
An hour later
I have done
A hundred little things
I had meant to do all week.

I think I get
My energy
From loving you.

Can it be
Love charges me?

One thing more.
I think
The sink
Is working better, too.

YOU AND ME? DON'T BE SILLY

Out of all the possibilities for love
How strange it should be us.
>   You with no backhand.
>   Me with no forethought.

>   Low-keyed you.
>   Over-wrought me.

I am still not sure
What brought us together.
>   Accidental touching?
>   Planned encounters?

I did not think I was looking for love, my dear.
Maybe that is why I found it.

SETTLING IN

I have settled into love
The way that houses settle
        Plaster slightly cracked
        Floors a little tilted

But still this love is home.

It's really rather sweet
A kind of fire-in-the-fireplace love
        Charred a little
        Singed from time to time

But still this love burns strong.

I do not know. Maybe this is all
That I will ever have
A sort of old house slow fire love,
But it gives me such pleasure
That I do not long for Roman candles.

For in the joining, in the sweetness,
In the holding of our love
There is no sense of strangeness.
There is no dislocation,
For no matter where we are
If we're together, it is home.
And look, my dear, just over there—
I think I see a Roman candle.

I LOVE YOU

So there we were
Wrapped in each other.
Wrapped.
Tied.
Knotted.
Rapt.
You did not speak
When you looked at me.
At least you said nothing I could hear,
But in eighteen languages I saw you say
I love you.

True marriage
is not my devotion
to you,
nor is it
yours to me.
True marriage
is our devotion
to us.

SONG OF LOVE

I have loved you to the rhythm of a rain that knows no end.
I have loved you to the sounds of a town that never sleeps.
I have loved you to the music of a rustling, raging wind.
I have loved you after time ran out on both your watch and mine.
I have loved you 'til my body was a single singing star
And so it is and so it is it is it is
For I love you to the beat of a love that will not quit.

AND OTHER SIGNS OF LOVE

Most loves are judged
By outward signs
      I
          kiss kiss
     love
        pat pat
  you
        touch touch
  yes.

But a kiss pat touch
That flowers first
Is not the sign of love that lasts.

For love puts down its roots
Long after there are blossoms.
You see, my dear,
Nature is not always what it seems.

Lois Wyse's first book of poetry,
Love Poems for the Very Married (1967), and the two that followed
Are You Sure You Love Me (1969),
and *I Love You Better Now* (1971)
established her as the leading contemporary love poet.
She has since written two more books
on the man/woman relationship,
A Weeping Eye Can Never See (1972),
and *Lovetalk* (1973).